m.
With Christ
mas!
2018

Love
Carol

THE BATTLE OF FRANKLIN

THE
BATTLE
OF
FRANKLIN
★
A TALE OF A HOUSE DIVIDED

Original Stageplay by
A. S. PETERSON

Songs by PATRICK THOMAS

Also by A. S. PETERSON

FIN'S REVOLUTION

BOOK 1: THE FIDDLER'S GUN
"A soulful, instant classic."
—Allan Heinberg, Screenwriter of WONDER WOMAN

BOOK 2: FIDDLER'S GREEN
"Inventive, engaging, unpredictable. Peterson's prose sparkles with life."
—Douglas McKelvey, author of THE ANGEL KNEW PAPA AND THE DOG

TALES OF AN UNREMEMBERED COUNTRY

THE TIMELY ARRIVAL OF BARNABAS BEAD

THE ORACLE OF PHILADELPHIA

INTRODUCTION

WHEN DIRECTOR MATT LOGAN at Studio Tenn asked me to write an original stage play about the Battle of Franklin, and I immediately said yes. Then I went home and thought: *What have I done?*

In the tale of Tod Carter and the Carter House, we'd found a great story, a great cast of characters, and a wealth of perspectives from which to view the battle. But with only a handful of actors and actresses, how was I to go about presenting the breadth, depth, and complexity of a battle that involved tens of thousands of men and left thousands of them wounded and dead? Was it even possible to convey the enormity of such a thing on stage?

In my effort to answer those questions, I began digging, excavating the story, looking for its bones. I toured the Carter House. I read letter after letter written by the soldiers and families that lived in the area and knew the battle firsthand. I read every known word Tod Carter ever wrote or published. I read books like Eric Jacobson's excellent *For Cause and for Country*. I asked questions. Who were these people? How did they think? How did they see one another?

Slowly, I began to inhabit the characters and bring them to life. Fountain Branch Carter—aging, intractable, bereaved. Tod Carter—smart, principled, clever. Mary Alice McPhail—alone, caring for her father, desperate for a family at peace. Calphurnia Carter—a slave caught in the no-man's land between freedom and bondage. General Jacob Cox—war weary, disillusioned, homesick.

I found what I always find when I write: that characters—whether fictional or real—are most alive when we see the complex ways in which they've been broken and the unlooked-for ways in which they might be made whole once more. So I peeled these characters open to see what might be hiding beneath the surface. By necessity, some in the show are fictional and some are composites, but I think the characters we've chosen to bring to life provide a complex snapshot of the real men and women who shouldered the weight of the Civil War.

I came to see that while the Battle of Franklin was fought with muskets and cannons, fists and swords, it was also fought in hearts and souls, between fathers and sons, between masters and slaves, between brothers and sisters. The battle itself was the vast backdrop for an intimate war raging between people who claimed to love one another but were blinded by their own illusions or ideals.

The answer, then, to my question of how to convey the epic scale of the Battle of Franklin was this: Tell the human story. Meticulous details of battle lines and troop formations may be riveting to many, but the personal stories of the men and women who saw the war and lived and died in it—that's something everyone can connect with.

The job of the writer is to open the viewer's eyes to the perspectives at work in the story. Confederate, Unionist, slave— they each bring something different to the battlefield, and if we can understand what led them there, maybe we can learn to understand them as humans rather than as mere clichés or stereotypes.

In the final analysis, *The Battle of Franklin* isn't just about the Civil War; it's about the absence of civility in mankind—in all of us. If we can tell that story well, then the details of the battle fall into place, because the battlefield isn't merely a stretch of grass outside Franklin, Tennessee; the battlefield is the wrecked plain of the human heart, and we are all, in some measure, combatants.

In remembering the story of the Carter House and the Battle of Franklin, by mounting that remembrance in the form of a stage play, we're bearing witness to a history we're forever in danger of repeating—and in remembering these stories we may yet find ways to resolve the past into a more civil future.

CAST

MINT JULEP (TOD CARTER) – a saucy young man in his 20s

HENRY CARTER – a slave the same age as Mint Julep

FOUNTAIN CARTER (FB) – A noble/tough old man in his 60s

CALLIE CARTER – slave and wife of Henry

MARY ALICE MCPHAIL – older sister (30s) to Tod Carter

ALBERT LOTZ – German immigrant, middle-aged

RETHA LOTZ – wife of Albert, also German

GENERAL COX – Union General, tall, war weary, and exhausted

SAMUELS – Union aide to General Cox, a stooge

COLONEL MOSCOE – a confederate recruiting officer

SOLDIER 1 – Soldiers will play both Union and Rebels at various points

SOLDIER 2

ACT I

SCENE 1

Mint Julep enters the stage via a bridge that stretches out of the darkness. He looks around and begins to pull furniture together, creating a room. At the center is a bed, which he ponders thoughtfully before turning to the audience.

MINT JULEP: Time is a circle, isn't it? A wheel. It spins us, tumbles us. Again and again, rolling us down lanes of loss, along byways of consequence, across intersections of unity and division, preservation and destruction.

As Mint talks, the cast slowly enters from the bridge and walks around the set, reminding themselves of its use and putting on clothes and uniforms.

SONG: "WE ARE CLIMBING JACOB'S LADDER"

WE ARE CLIMBING JACOB'S LADDER
WE ARE CLIMBING JACOB'S LADDER
WE ARE CLIMBING JACOB'S LADDER
SOLDIERS OF THE CROSS

During the song, the cast separates into factions: Union, Confederate, Slave.

MINT JULEP: Time rolls ever on as we repeat our forgotten histories, and in its turn it reveals the fateful freedoms that bind and keep us. It brings us face to face with all we try so hard to push away, until, in a whorl of apocalyptic vision, we see clearly—if only for a moment—and do our best to remember what we've seen.

Isn't that right, brothers and sisters?

COMPANY: Yes, sir. Mmmm. Mmmm. Let it be.

MINT JULEP: But the rolling by of time and our memories of its passage are never the same. No, sir. Memory haunts time, peoples its halls with—

FB: Regret.

GENERAL COX: Doubt.

CALLIE: Grief.

MINT JULEP: Memory is an instrument of the soul, not subject to the cold legalities of physics or geography. And what are our histories but a twining together of time and memory like two complementary yarns.

Round and round we wind them. Round and round we turn. Always something new. Always something old.

These faces, this night, this house. All . . . familiar. Like something far off come dancing near, something just at the edge of sight.

Characters step out into the light then back into shadow.

MARY ALICE: Tod, not like this! Come back!

CALLIE: Don't close the door, Marse Carter! Don't close it!

FB: Come back! Come back! What must I say?

HENRY: Thenceforward and forever . . .

MINT JULEP: Snatches of memory coalescing into the firmness
                 of history. Do you see it too?

COMPANY: Mmmm. Hmmm. Yes, brother.

MINT JULEP: But how do I tell the tale of it all? A tale—

FB: Of fathers and sons divided.

MARY ALICE: Of men and women entangled by bonds they
                 cannot see and will not cut.

MINT JULEP: How do I tell the merest detail, but to say it's a
                 tale—

CALLIE: Of a broken family.

GENERAL COX: A family at war with itself.

HENRY: Tomorrow the Master will come to gather his
                 sheaves—

FB: —to reap what we have sown.

MINT JULEP: And we are here to bear witness.

                 Say, brothers, sisters, will you come with me
                 once more?

COMPANY: Yes, brother. Mmmm. Hmm. Take us there.

MINT JULEP: Allow me an introduction.

Call me Mint Julep.

A *nom de plume*, if you will. In another turn of the wheel, I reported for a rebel newspaper, and my public enjoyed a saucy moniker—not to mention it kept the Yanks off my scent.

You keep close. A great blow shall soon be struck, and we all shall tremble in its wake. Do you hear the wheels of time creaking to life? Come with me, and we will ride it back into memory.

I, Mint Julep, shall be your guide.

Scene 2

The Carter House.

MINT JULEP: Here we are. The house of Fountain Branch Carter, wellspring of a veritable river of Carters. It's a fine home built on a fair patch of grass in the Tennessee hills. A good place to be. Good as any I ever saw.

There's Mary Alice, eldest daughter and woman of the household. Look at her! I'd forgot how pretty she was then. It's a year yet before she'll marry, and nearly ten before she'll see her husband off to join the Cause.

FB: There was a boy lived here too.

MARY ALICE: A golden boy named . . .

MINT JULEP: Tod Carter. I knew him well. Smart kid—and good looking too. *(Winks)*

He was born right over there in that bed.

FB: He grew up out in those hills.

MARY ALICE: He learned to hunt rabbits and squirrels in those woods.

HENRY: He fished out of the Harpeth and climbed the trees in that orchard.

MINT JULEP: I remember. Ever climbing up, up, high as he could get, trying to reach for something just beyond him. Could be that's still the case, come to think on it.

              I expect he'll show up before long.

Mint steps aside to watch as the scene begins.

MARY ALICE: You could at least call on her, papa.

FB: I told your mother when I married her: I'll only wed once. I don't intend that death should alter that vow.

MARY ALICE: All I'm saying is that there's no sense in widow Johnson being lonely there and you being lonely here—when you could both be lonely together.

FB: The farm is my business now. As are you and Tod. I don't need anyone else to complicate the matter.

MARY ALICE: But, Papa, if you'd just let me ask her to dinner.

FB: Enough, Mary Alice. I've given my answer.

MARY ALICE: She's a fine dancer, you know?

FB gives Mary Alice a baleful look.

              All right, all right. Tod? Tod, come in here. It's time for your dinner.

Mint Julep looks around.

MARY ALICE: Tod? Tod!

MINT JULEP: I'll play the part.

Mint Julep doffs his hat and smooths his hair down.

MINT JULEP: Here I am.

MARY ALICE: Sit down. Where on earth have you been all afternoon.

MINT JULEP: Me and Henry was fishing.

FB: Fishing?

MINT JULEP: Yes, sir. Henry caught a catfish. He put it in a bucket so he can keep it for a pet.

                You want me to show it to you, Pa? I ain't never seen a catfish so—

FB: I thought you were working on your writing with Mrs. Lotz.

Mint Julep looks around sheepishly.

                Well?

MINT JULEP: Sorry, Pa. I forgot.

MARY ALICE: You forgot?

FB: I spend good money for those lessons. Yet you spend your time fishing instead. Very well. Tomorrow you can help Henry clear the south field.

MINT JULEP: But you said I could come with you to town tomorrow!

FB: Yes, I did. And you said you would take your
                lessons from Mrs. Lotz. You've changed your
                mind, and now so must I.

MINT JULEP: But, Pa—

MARY ALICE: Don't backtalk your papa.

MINT JULEP: It ain't fair! I don't even need her blame lessons.

FB: I have said all I have to say on the matter. Mary
                Alice would you pour me some milk?

MINT JULEP: It ain't fair—and I won't do it!

Mint Julep runs out in a huff.

MARY ALICE: Miss Retha won't have any trouble rescheduling
                his lesson, Papa. There's no harm done.

FB: He's old enough to do as he's told.

MARY ALICE: And young enough that he can't keep away from
                the river. He's just a boy, you know. He misses his
                mother. And he might want for a little affection
                from his father.

FB: It's time he started thinking like a man. And I
                would appreciate it if I did not have to explain
                my every decision to my eldest daughter.

MARY ALICE: Well who else is going to talk any sense into you?

                I'll explain it all to Miss Retha in the morning.

Mint enters as the scene changes to the exterior of the house.

MINT JULEP: Hardly ten years old. I tell you a boy that age
                thinks he can smell an unfair word at fifty paces.

He'll kick and holler at a stone if he thinks he's been mistreated by it, and FB is nothing if not a rock. Grey, hard, settled, and stubborn. Just the kind of obstacle a boy can break himself against. And the boy will try, over and over and over again.

Henry, a young slave boy, enters.

HENRY: Tod! Tod, where you at?

MINT JULEP: Well look who it is! That's ol' Henry Carter!

FB: Bought his mother off the block in Mobile while she was still carrying him. She was never worth much, but Henry was a strong boy, a fine investment—born just two weeks after Tod.

MINT JULEP: Though he hardly ever had a sensible thought in his head.

HENRY: Tod? That you?

Mint snatches off his hat.

MINT JULEP: Hey, Henry.

HENRY: Come on let's go back to the river. Got to get me another catfish.

MINT JULEP: Another one? You jest got one big as you are.

HENRY: Got to catch another one so Dog don't be lonely.

MINT JULEP: Dog?

HENRY: Yep. I name him "Dog" on account of I keeping him for a pet.

MINT JULEP: It's only a fool would name a catfish "Dog,"
               Henry. Besides, I ain't going to no river.

HENRY: What got you so sore?

MINT JULEP: Tell me something, Henry. Ain't you tired of this
               place? Tired of milking them cows? Fetching
               that water?

HENRY: Yeah. I guess.

MINT JULEP: Ain't you tired of listening to Pa gloat over his
               fancy cotton gin and always telling folks how to
               do?

HENRY: I guess.

MINT JULEP: You know what I'm tired of?

HENRY: I guess you tired of fishing at the river.

MINT JULEP: Nope. I'm tired of folks trying to give me
               lessons—and that's just the start of it.

HENRY: Lessons? Ain't nobody ever give me no lessons.
               What they look like?

MINT JULEP: Pa's always after me to take lessons for some-
               thing. He wants Miss Retha to learn me to write,
               but I already know it. What's the point of lessons
               for a thing when you already know it?

HENRY: How you know it?

MINT JULEP: Pa learned me to write since I was a baby. Only
               he thinks Miss Retha can do it better. But she
               don't even talk right! She can't learn me no
               letters. And besides, it ain't fair for a body to be

told what to do. I got rights, you know?

HENRY: What's rights?

MINT JULEP: What's rights? You don't know nothing, Henry.
              It means somebody can't tell you to do some-
              thing if you don't want to do it. That's rights. I
              got em. Everybody got em.

HENRY: Well, I ain't never seen 'em.

MINT JULEP: They're hard to see, I reckon, but I got em. Every-
              body does.

*Henry inspects his arms and body, as if he might find a spot or a
tear, looking to see if he's got rights like Tod.*

              Only Pa thinks he can take mine.

HENRY: That why you sore?

MINT JULEP: I told you, I ain't sore. I just got rights is all.

HENRY: You seem right sore.

MINT JULEP: Let's run away, Henry.

HENRY: My Lord! Where would we go?

MINT JULEP: We could go to Nashville. Naw, that ain't far, and
              I been there last year.

HENRY: How about Atlanta?

MINT JULEP: Naw. Everbody wants to go to Atlanta. If I'm to
              run away, I want to go somewhere far off. Some-
              where most folks ain't never been.

HENRY: Like England?

MINT JULEP: What? I ain't going to no England. Kings takes even more rights than Pa does. That's how come great-granddaddy fit the Revolution.

HENRY: Fit the what?

MINT JULEP: Nevermind. I know where we can go. Somewhere Pa won't never come looking. And I hear they got rights to do whatever they want, whenever they want.

HENRY: Where's that?

MINT JULEP: Hell.

HENRY: Hell?

MINT JULEP: Pa told me I was going there anyway.

HENRY: I spect he was just sore is all.

MINT JULEP: Let's do it. Let's go to hell, Henry. It can't be no hotter than it is in Atlanta.

HENRY: Well, all right. But where is it?

MINT JULEP: South, I guess. Come on.

                            INSTRUMENTAL

SCENE 3

Mint puts his hat back on and address the audience as the scene changes.

MINT JULEP: They made it about three miles down the Columbia Turnpike. Not bad for boys of that age. But when the old man got hold of them, he wore Tod out. Henry too.

FB: They were thick as thieves in those days.

MINT JULEP: A child looks and sees nothing more or less than another child. It takes a man to whisper in his ear, and color in the difference.

FB: By the time they'd grown, everything had changed.

MINT JULEP: The word "secession" had taken shape and it haunted the dinner tables of Tennessee, until in June of 1861 it took on flesh and blood and was a ghost no longer.

               Look now!

A crowd cheers and rushes out.

HENRY:	Marse Tod, what all the fuss?
MINT JULEP:	Fuss? It ain't no fuss, Henry. It's a celebration.
HENRY:	Somebody birthday?
MINT JULEP:	Good Lord, Henry. Just be quiet and watch.
FB:	Quiet! Quiet!
CROWD:	Read it!
FB:	*(Grimly)* We have a telegram here from Nashville. It says: We, the people of the State of Tennessee, asserting the right, as a free and independent people, do ordain and declare that all the laws and ordinances by which the State of Tennessee became a member of the United States of America are hereby annulled.
CROWD:	*(cheers)*
HENRY:	What it mean, Marse Tod?
MINT JULEP:	It means we're free people, Henry. And Abraham Lincoln can stuff his federal gov'met in his own ...
CROWD:	Raise the flag!
HENRY:	His own what?
MINT JULEP:	Give me that.

Mint takes the flag from a member of the crowd and runs to the front.

	Ladies and gentlemen, quiet now. Hush.
FB:	What are you doing?

CROWD: Raise it up!

MINT JULEP: Today being the fine, momentous day that it is, I feel sure we should mark it with some symbolic gesture.

CROWD: Raise it! Run it up! Run it up!

MINT JULEP: How would y'all like it if we tear down Abe Lincoln's rag?

FB: Tod! Enough.

CROWD: Tear it down!

Tod hauls Old Glory down the flag pole and tosses it to the crowd who tear it apart and cheer.

MINT JULEP: What do you say we run up a new flag?

CROWD: Run it up!

Tod runs up the confederate flag amid raucous cheering.

MINT JULEP: You know what that is? That's liberty. We got rights, ain't we? And will Abe Lincoln be the one to take em away?

CROWD: No!

The scene freezes.

FB: I never saw a boy so got up with self-righteousness and indignation.

GENERAL COX: It's like a madness arose from the earth and clouded the air. Blinded him. Blinded people by the thousands.

MINT JULEP: When we're blind, how do we choose when we
               come to the fork in the path? How do we see
               where it goes or where it ends?

HENRY: We all start out for the river—

MINT JULEP: But by unseen turns we stray into the mire.

Mint rejoins the scene.

               Colonel Moscoe! Have you got enlistment
               papers?

COLONEL: I do indeed. Step right up, young man.

FB: Thank you, colonel, but there's no need.

MINT JULEP: Let go of me.

FB: The army has plenty of boys to fill it. It doesn't
               need any more of mine.

MINT JULEP: Any more of yours? You don't own me.

MARY ALICE: Tod, please! Don't make a fuss.

FB: You are needed at home, and there's an end to it.

MINT JULEP: The farm's got plenty of old men and women and
               slaves to keep it. It's the war that needs me, or
               there won't be a farm left.

FB: We will discuss this later. Come.

MINT JULEP: If you had any pride you'd sign up along with me
               instead of trying to hold me out of it. Let me go!

MARY ALICE: Don't, Tod. Not like this. You'll embarrass us.

MINT JULEP: I'll embarrass you?

MARY ALICE: You're being selfish. Papa can't take care of the farm without you. At least come home and let's talk about it.

FB: Come, Mary Alice. If your brother wishes to be a fool, leave him to it.

MINT JULEP: There's a Yankee army mustered and ready to take every inch of our farm, and you won't even stand up to help defend it. I'd rather be thought a fool than a coward.

MARY ALICE: Your mouth! Keep your voice down. And calling names isn't helping, Papa. Can we go home and discuss this in private?

MINT JULEP: Hey, Henry!

HENRY: Talking to me, Marse Tod?

MINT JULEP: I said "Henry" didn't I? You know how to plow a field, don't you?

HENRY: Yes sir.

MARY ALICE: Tod . . .

MINT JULEP: And you know how to bring in the cotton, and how to work the gin?

HENRY: I spect so.

MINT JULEP: Well there you go. You don't need me at all.

FB: Henry, go on and fetch the wagon.

MARY ALICE: There's more to keeping a family than plowing a field and bringing in cotton, and you know it.

MINT JULEP:	And there's more to keeping a country than staying home with the slaves and women.
MARY ALICE:	Tod!
MINT JULEP:	Colonel, give me a pen and show me where to put it. And may every man of a good conscience follow after.
COLONEL:	Sign right here, Mr. Carter.
MARY ALICE:	Tod, wait . . .
FB:	Leave him to it.
COLONEL:	Ma'am, the boy is of age, is he not?
MARY ALICE:	He is, but . . .
COLONEL:	Then I advise you leave him in the able care of the Confederacy. We round up enough like him and this business won't last long. Maybe even get him home by Christmas.
MINT JULEP:	You hear that? Back by Christmas. Don't wait up.
MARY ALICE:	It's not right to go off with bad words between us. Tod? Please?
FB:	Let him be. Maybe the army will make a man out of him.

Mint and a gaggle of young men sign up, put on gray caps and march off stage singing. Mint steps out of the parade and watches.

SONG: "JOHNNY COMES MARCHING HOME"

MINT JULEP:	Yonder he goes. Soon to be a Confederate captain . . . same as yours truly. *(winks)*

GENERAL COX: He thought Billy Yank would bend over like tall grass and give way before the rush of all that Southern pride.

MARY ALICE: Back home by Christmas?

MINT JULEP: He believed it so hard he thought he could make it so.

FB: And so did his father.

SCENE 4

Interior. The Carter House. Mary Alice enters.

MARY ALICE: Papa? Papa! Come quick.

CALLIE: Goodness, Miss Mary. What you hollering for?

The scene freezes.

MINT JULEP: Callie Carter. She and Henry married some years back. Though some didn't allow such formality between slaves, FB did in Henry's case. He liked that boy—and Henry liked Callie.

The scene resumes.

MARY ALICE: Callie, it's a letter from Tod. Where's Papa? I don't dare open it unless Papa's here.

CALLIE: He down at the gin. Spect they'll be up for lunch for too long.

MARY ALICE: Run and fetch him, Callie. He won't want to wait when there's a letter. Go on, now.

CALLIE: Yes, ma'am.

Callie exits as Henry enters.

HENRY: Where you goan, Callie? Where she goan, Miss
                Mary?

MARY ALICE: She's gone to fetch Papa. There's a letter from
                Tod. Isn't that wonderful, Henry?

HENRY: I spect so. Sure glad he ain't come back like
                Mister David's. Heard all three his boys come
                home dead from a scuffle at Fort Donelson.

MARY ALICE: Oh, it's awful!

HENRY: Terrible. Yes, ma'am.

MARY ALICE: We hear the worst news. Worse every day, it
                seems. I do worry over him, Henry.

HENRY: Yes, ma'am.

MARY ALICE: And I worry about Papa as much as Tod. Do you
                know he has not sent Tod a single letter in all
                this time? A whole year and not even one! He
                says he can't bear to think of him in danger, but
                I know better. It's stubborness is all. They're so
                thick-headed—both of them. It's a character
                flaw, Henry. Stubbornness.

HENRY: I spect so. Marse Carter tole me come find you.
                He ask could you see some food get sent out
                to the gin. He want to get finished for the rain
                come.

Callie enters.

CALLIE: He on his way, Miss Mary. His leg ailing him
                again so he tole me to come on ahead. He

wouldn't be fetched at all till I tole him they was a letter.

MARY ALICE: Henry, you help Callie.

HENRY: I sure hope that letter from Marse Tod got some good news. I worries about him myself sometime.

MARY ALICE: Why thank you, Henry. Do you see what good manners he has got, Callie?

CALLIE: Mmmm hmmm.

FB enters.

MARY ALICE: Papa! Look we've got a letter.

FB takes the letter.

Why, I'm about to burst waiting to open it.

FB: Mattie Thompson got a letter two days ago from her boy, Harmon. He was wounded in Antietam and lost both arms.

MARY ALICE: My word. But it's Tod's handwriting on the envelope, so he can't have lost his arms, can he?

FB: I suppose that's true at least.

FB sits and opens the letter.

MARY ALICE: What's it say, Papa.

FB: "Dear Mary Alice and family" ... he doesn't even address me.

MARY ALICE: Hush, Papa, I'm sure he doesn't mean it that way. Go on and read it.

MINT JULEP: "We are not doing anything much here. It is so muddy and bad weather that we don't drill any at all. I have begun as a war correspondent for the newspaper, and we have word of great victories at Fredericksburg and Harper's Ferry. It gives us all confidence that this war will soon be ended. I would like to come home soon but the general says we may be needed at any moment.

              It is ever on our minds that the Yanks have occupied the country about our home, and we pray you do not suffer overmuch from their depredations. It was to prevent such aggression that I left you, and it is only with success that I shall return.

              I miss you all and think of you often. Tell the darkies that I am well and they need not worry. Tell father I am an aide now to the general, and I believe he prizes my help dearly."

FB: "Your brother, Theodrick Carter."

MARY ALICE: Well that's good, Papa. It's good, right?

FB: Good news for this general, perhaps.

MARY ALICE: Well if he got a promotion he must be doing just fine. And a general's aide sounds like safer work than some I've heard.

FB: I dreamed of him, Mary.

MARY ALICE: What? Of Tod?

As FB speaks the others slowly turn away from him.

FB:	He was here, and your mother was here too. Everyone was. And we seemed happy together. But no one would look at anyone else. There were no faces.
	No matter where I looked, the faces were turned away from me, and from one another.
	I couldn't see them. Any of them.

The others turn back toward FB.

MARY ALICE:	What do you think it means?
HENRY:	Pardon me, Marse Carter. I goan ride down to the gin to feed the boys. Thought you might want to ride along, give that bad leg a rest. Rain coming on fast.
FB:	Thank you, Henry. I'll be right out.
HENRY:	I'm sure Marse Tod be all right.
FB:	Help me up, Henry. Give me your hand.

Henry helps FB out of his chair.

MARY ALICE:	Thank you, Henry. Don't let him work too hard.
HENRY:	No, ma'am. He got to take care himself till Marse Tod get back. I bet he don't be gone too much longer. He'll whup them Yanks quick to get back home. Spect he already got a plan to do it.
MARY ALICE:	I expect he does.

FB sits at the edge of the stage.

| HENRY: | You keep inside, Miss Mary, so you don't catch sick. |

MARY ALICE: Don't let him get caught in the rain. He's too old
               for it.

Henry exits.

MINT JULEP: I never expected the old man to get so—old.
               People change so much and so fast—but they
               stay just the same. It's funny, ain't it?

MARY ALICE: Go on, Henry. Tell them boys to get moving
               before they get wet.

MINT JULEP: I haven't got the heart to tell them what's coming.

GENERAL COX: It's a mighty storm gathering up with a wail of
               wind and a fateful show of lightning.

MINT JULEP: Coming right this way too. The river is likely to
               be swole up for a week.

               Home by Christmas. Wouldn't that have been
               something.

GENERAL COX: Even those who do come home are broken in
               one way or another.

MINT JULEP: It's few indeed will come home whole.

               SONG: "I WILL COMFORT THEE"

*While Mary Alice sings, FB picks up Tod's letter and reads it silently.
Mary tends the house around him. At the end of the song, FB sham-
bles offstage as Mary Alice sits and reads the letter to herself.*

SCENE 5

A knock at the door.

CALLIE: Why good afternoon, Miss Retha.

RETHA: Hello, Callie.

CALLIE: Miss Mary, it's Miss Retha come to visit.

MARY ALICE: Come right on inside, Retha. How are you?

RETHA: I have been banished. Again.

CALLIE: I'll fetch some buttermilk.

MARY ALICE: Thank you, Callie.

RETHA: Banished! Albert has forbidden me to play my own violin in my own house. Says it "troubles his mind." Pah! His mind.

MARY ALICE: Well, you're welcome to come and play for us any time. You could practice in the cellar, if you like.

RETHA: I will give him trouble, and I will trouble more than his mind.

MARY ALICE: Well I doubt it takes much to trouble such a feeble instrument.

RETHA: This is why I like you, Mary Alice. You understand the difficulty of a husband.

MARY ALICE: I don't know that anyone understands entirely. I haven't seen mine in better than a year and I find myself missing even our difficulties.

RETHA: I am sorry, Mary Alice. I have been thoughtless.

MARY ALICE: No, no, it's fine, Retha. We had a letter from Tod today, did you hear?

RETHA: How wonderful!

MARY ALICE: He's fine to hear him tell it. Even got himself a promotion.

RETHA: A promotion? My goodness, he has done well, hasn't he?

MARY ALICE: He's working for a general now. Which I'm glad of, I don't mind telling you.

               He addressed the letter to me again.

RETHA: Again? Poor FB.

MARY ALICE: It's like he won't even speak to Papa.

RETHA: Hmmph. Boys.

MARY ALICE: You expect a boy to be unreasonable, but it's Papa I can't understand.

RETHA: Hmmph. Men!

MARY ALICE: Can I tell you something, Retha?

RETHA: Of course.

MARY ALICE: I don't think Tod would have joined the army if
              Papa hadn't been there watching.

RETHA: What do you mean?

MARY ALICE: I remember once when Tod was a boy, Papa sent
              him over to your house to work with Albert for
              the afternoon. I think Papa had it in mind that
              Albert might teach him some of the carpentry
              trade.

RETHA: I remember it. He was adorable. Tod, I mean,
              not Albert. Yi!

MARY ALICE: Well, Albert showed him how to make a little
              drum box, and he was completely taken with the
              thing. Tod ran to show Papa and banged on the
              drum as hard as he could.

RETHA: Ah, boys.

MARY ALICE: And Papa was sharp with him. Told him to stop
              raising the dead with his noise. But Tod wanted
              Papa to love the thing as hard as he did and he
              wouldn't stop. He beat the drum until he broke
              to pieces. Then he stormed out while Papa threw
              it on the fire.

              I don't know if that makes any sense, but that's
              how it felt when Tod went off to the army, like
              he'd smashed another drum.

Callie enters and pours buttermilk.

MARY ALICE: Thank you, Callie.

RETHA: Thank you, Callie.

MARY ALICE: Callie's the one that has it figured out you know, Retha?

RETHA: Oh, does she?

CALLIE: What's that, Miss Mary?

MARY ALICE: That Henry of hers is perfectly sensible. He does just what he's told and doesn't ever give anyone any trouble. Isn't that right, Callie?

CALLIE: I reckon so, Miss Mary.

RETHA: Henry would never banish me.

MARY ALICE: Or run off and leave us. Callie, you must tell us one day how you've done it.

CALLIE: I don't know, Miss Mary.

MARY ALICE: Maybe we should go get us one just like him, Retha. We could have us a man who would stay home and keep quiet and do just as he's asked.

RETHA: It will be a scandal.

MARY ALICE: What do you think, Callie. Where can we get us another one like Henry?

CALLIE: I don't know, ma'am. I got to get back to the kitchen if you don't need nothing else.

MARY ALICE: Of course, Callie.

RETHA: And I'd better go as well. Albert will begin to hope I've left him.

MARY ALICE: You're awful, Retha.

RETHA: I know.

MARY ALICE: The both of you should come for dinner sometime soon.

RETHA: We would like that. I will talk to Albert.

MARY ALICE: And you tell him I adore your fiddle playing.
He's welcome to banish you to our cellar any
time.

RETHA: Hah!

Retha and Mary Alice exit.

Scene 6

Henry and Callie enter.

HENRY: Why you sneakin' around, Callie?

CALLIE: I ain't sneakin', but I got to show you something.

Callie pulls a folded paper out of her apron and shows it to Henry.

HENRY: That's mighty big words. I ain't no good with them kind. What it say?

CALLIE: It's from the president.

HENRY: Ol' Jeff Davis?

CALLIE: No. The *president*. And it say slaves is freed.

HENRY: Lord. You sure?

CALLIE: Yes, I'm sure. Look here. It says: "all persons held as slaves shall be thenceforward and forever free." And it's signed by . . .

HENRY: *(sounding out the name)* Ab-ra-ham Lin-coln. Where you get this?

CALLIE: Sally's boy run it over last night on account of

they ain't nobody wants us to see it.

HENRY: My Lord. Marse Carter know about it?

CALLIE: Well, I don't know, but I spect he does.

HENRY: I don't think he like it too much if he does.

CALLIE: Well what are we going to do, Henry?

HENRY: Do? Do bout what?

CALLIE: Did you just see what I tole you? If slaves is free why ain't Marse Carter say nothing about it? Don't that make you think? Maybe we belong to leave.

HENRY: Leave? Where we goan go? We leave, what Marse Carter going to do? He cain't get that cotton in by hisself.

CALLIE: Well maybe we go north? I heard up north they got negro folks has houses of they own, and schools for they chirren.

HENRY: I don't know about no north, Callie. I don't know bout nothing but here. I ain't never been no futher than that river yonder. I cain't swim no how.

CALLIE: They got bridges for rivers, Henry. What's wrong with you?

HENRY: Ain't nuthin' wrong with me. I just don't know about no papers from presidents. I don't know but one way to be—and I'm being it.

            Marse Carter a good man. Don't seem right to

run off from him. Maybe we ask him what he think.

CALLIE: Ask him!? Ask him what? Ask him can you run off? What is in that head of yours, Henry Carter. Ask him? I'd like to see that.

FB enters.

CALLIE: Evening, Marse Carter. Dinner is nearly done cooking. Coffee ready.

FB pours some coffee.

FB: It sure does smell fine, Callie. You helping with dinner this evening, Henry?

HENRY: No, sir. Callie was showing me—

Callie elbows him.

CALLIE: I was just showing him that new china Miss Mary got for when the ladies come after church next week.

FB: Well what's that you got there, Henry. You practicing your letters? How many times have I tried to teach this boy to read, Callie? He just don't seem to take to it. Let me see what you got there?

FB takes the proclamation.

FB: Now where'd you come by this, Henry.

HENRY: Callie, give it to me, sir.

FB: Course she did. Well, do you know what it says.

HENRY: I cain't read it too good, but Callie shown me

	where it says that slaves is th-thenceforward and forever free.
FB:	Hmm ... yes, it does indeed say that. But did you see who signed it?
HENRY:	Yes, sir. Abraham Lincoln, sir.
FB:	And is Abraham Lincoln the president of the Confederate States?
HENRY:	No ... no, sir.
FB:	It's all right, Henry. I understand. But the fact is Tennessee does not recognize the authority of Abraham Lincoln. And this proclamation of his frees only runaways and slaves in a few states where he has no say in the matter.
	I'm sorry, Henry. But this paper is meaningless.
HENRY:	Yes, sir.
FB:	I've always been good to you and your family, haven't I?
HENRY:	Yes, sir.
CALLIE:	Oh, yes sir.
FB:	How would my children and grandchildren live if I didn't have your help with the farm?
HENRY:	Don't know, sir.
FB:	You're a good boy, Henry. I think of you, all of you, as my very own. You know that don't you?
HENRY:	Yes, sir.

FB: Do you know where Tod is right now?

Henry: He gone to fight, sir.

FB: That's right. Gone to fight. My own son has put himself at hazard to protect us. To protect you too, Henry. You wouldn't want to betray that sacrifice would you?

Henry: No, sir.

FB: Then we don't need this, do we?

FB holds out the paper.

Henry: I spect not, sir.

FB: Go on and tear it up.

Henry: Marse Carter, I . . .

FB: That's okay, now. No need to apologize. Just tear it up and let's put it behind us.

Callie: Henry . . .

Henry tears up the paper.

FB: Those biscuits sure do smell fine. Henry, why don't you help Callie with the table. You eat with us this evening. We'll ride out to the gin first thing in the morning and get the rest of that crop baled.

Henry: Yes, sir.

FB exits. Mint Julep comes out to watch the scene.

Callie: Henry . . .

HENRY: Marse Carter right, Callie. He always been good
           to us. He give us to eat. He give us a house to live
           in. Give us clothes to wear. He invite us to dinner
           in his house. He treat us like we his own.

CALLIE: But we ain't, Henry. I ain't. You ain't. Our chirren
           ain't. What happens when they get too grown
           and Marse Carter need to send them off some-
           where else? Then they be somebody else's own.
           You want that?

HENRY: Callie, I don't know. You hear him. He say this
           ain't nothing to do with us round here. It don't
           matter.

CALLIE: Well then maybe we get up yonder and we can
           get somewhere it does matter, Henry. You know
           what else? Once a man is free that man can fight.

HENRY: What you talking about, Callie.

CALLIE: That paper say a black man can jine the army
           now. Marse Carter say freedom ain't for black
           folks round here. Maybe there ain't but one way
           to make it so. A body got to fight, Henry. They's
           boys out there dying to see it so and oh, if I was
           a man, Henry, I'd fight. You'd never seen such a
           fight. But I ain't no man, and ain't nothing I can
           do to change that. But you, Henry—

HENRY: You want me to fight?

CALLIE: I ain't telling you what to do. I can't leave. Our
           chirren can't leave. But a strong black man could
           leave here and come back a free man. He could
           run off and fight for his chirren so his chirren

ain't got to be nobody else's own. And when he come back, he come back a fightin' man. Think of that? That man could have rights, Henry, and nobody tell him where to go no more. Nobody tell him bow his eyes and say "yes, marse," "no, marse." He be no body but his own.

HENRY: I ain't no fighting man, Callie. I don't know nuthin' but wagons and cotton and a little bit of carpenter work. Ain't none of that good for jining no army.

CALLIE: You are the foolest man, Henry. Never you mind. Forget I even shown you that paper. Come on with them biscuits.

FB and Mary Alice enter and sit at the table.

FB: Come sit down before those biscuits get cold.

Henry and Callie sit at a small table in the corner, apart from FB and Mary Alice.

FB: Let's give thanks. Bless, O Lord, these thy gifts which we are about to receive from thy bounty, through Christ, Our Lord . . . and bless, Lord, those who are parted from our table. Though we know they serve a righteous cause, hasten, O Lord, the day of their return. Amen.

Food is served in awkward silence.

MARY ALICE: Callie, did you see to the linens today?

CALLIE: Yes, ma'am. You want me mend that dress before bed? Might be we need to borrow a new needle from Miss Retha.

Mary Alice:	That's a fine idea, Callie. Why don't you go over and ask Miss Retha after dinner. I'll need the dress for church in the morning.
FB:	Henry's been working on his letters.
Mary Alice:	Have you, Henry?
Henry:	Yes, ma'am.
Mary Alice:	Before you know it, he'll be reading your books, Papa. He'll be expanding that mind of his. Getting ideas! What will you read, Henry?
Henry:	I don't know, ma'am.
FB:	I was just telling Henry what a good job he does. I don't know what we'd do without him. Do you, Mary Alice?
Mary Alice:	I hate to think of it. If it weren't for you and Callie we'd be run ragged and probably starve to death. I never did figure Tod would run off and leave us so long.
Henry:	*(mumbles)* He sure did run off . . .
FB:	What was that, Henry?
Henry:	Nothing, sir. Just wish Marse Tod ain't run off like he done.
FB:	He'll be home soon. The war can't last another year.
Mary Alice:	I know you miss him, Henry. But he's done a good thing. He's fighting for the Cause. And the Lord will see him safely home.

HENRY: Yes, ma'am.

Henry stands up.

                Marse Carter, I was thinking . . .

FB: Were you now? And what about?

HENRY: Maybe I go off to fight, like Marse Tod done.
                How would that be?

MARY ALICE: Why would you think such a thing, Henry?

HENRY: You say Marse Tod done a good thing. Maybe I
                do a good thing too.

CALLIE: Henry, sit yourself down and hush.

HENRY: It ain't nothing, Marse Carter. I jest was thinking.

FB: I see.

                Henry, put that thought out of your head. Your
                place is here, with us. You leave the fighting to
                Tod. The army is a white man's business, not
                yours. Do you understand?

HENRY: Yes, sir.

FB: Good, good. Was there anything else?

HENRY: No, sir.

                I best go get the gin closed up before it get dark.
                Other boys be waiting for me. Reckon they need
                somebody show 'em how to do.

FB: Tell them I'll be down directly to see it's done
                right.

HENRY: Yes, sir.

Henry picks the torn proclamation up from the table and walks out the door. Transition to exterior. Henry sings and runs away.

SONG: "RUN, RUN, RIVER (HENRY'S VERSION)"

FB walks across the stage calling for Henry.

FB: Henry? Henry! Come on, boy! Henry!

Scene 7

Mint Julep:	FB never could figure on why Henry run off. He couldn't account for it.
FB:	Considered some cherished bond to have been broken.
Mary Alice:	And he laid it all at the feet of the Union. The loss of Tod, the loss of Henry, and even his country.
Mint Julep:	When trouble visits us, that's what we do, isn't it?
FB:	We lay blame . . .
Mary Alice:	. . . and we lay it most harshly when we worry we may have invited the trouble ourselves.
FB:	We cast stones at our fellow men . . .
Albert:	. . . at our friends . . .
Mint Julep:	. . . at our sons . . .
FB:	. . . because we cannot bear to remove the stone within our own hearts.

GENERAL COX: As it goes with a family, so it goes with a nation. We hurl our stones until the only way back together is to pass through a hailstorm of our own making and pray it cleanses what it does not destroy entirely.

FB: The war we'd called up out of the darkness . . .

MINT JULEP: The war we'd summoned with our own cheers and parades and righteous madness . . . it began to consume us.

It spread from one end of the country to the other, until General Bobby Lee . . .

SOLDIER 1: . . . in whom we'd placed so much hope . . .

GENERAL COX: . . . was driven back at Gettysburg.

FB: From that day onward, the winds of desperation stirred.

ALBERT: They blew through Vicksburg . . .

RETHA: . . . through Chattanooga . . .

MARY ALICE: . . . through the bloody wilderness of Virginia . . .

MINT JULEP: . . . and a hundred other towns and valleys and fallow fields, leaving them each haunted by the bones of the dead . . .

CALLIE: . . . and the lamentations of the living.

MINT JULEP: And now, nearly three years after Tod Carter ran up his flag . . .

HENRY: . . . and a year since a slave run off . . .

GENERAL COX: . . . that bitter wind has come at last to trouble the hills of middle-Tennessee.

MINT JULEP: It's November 30th. The year of 1864. The wheel has tumbled us round and here we are again. I hear those awful winds a blowing. They're beginning to bend the trees and whistle in the hilltops. The lightning is sure to follow, and soon the thunder.

SOLDIER 2: Soon the hail.

FB: And soon the howl.

MINT JULEP: Yet amid it all—a light. A homecoming is at hand.

MARY ALICE: A moment for joy?

MINT JULEP: Perhaps?

FB: A moment of peace?

RETHA: Unlikely.

CALLIE: But a coming home to rest?

MINT JULEP: No doubt at all. For the long-departed have dreamt of home, and those loved and left have dreamt of reunion.

All these hopes and dreams shall be satisfied in one manner or another. But shall all manner of thing be well? Perhaps. Perhaps.

SCENE 8

FB Carter is asleep in bed. Someone pounds at the door. FB stirs. Pounding at the door again.

GENERAL COX: Open up!

FB sits up in bed, startled. More pounding and shouting. Mary Alice runs into the room. FB hurries out of bed and answers the door.

FB: What's the meaning of this!?

General Cox and Samuels burst in. Samuels is a greasy looking stooge of a lieutenant. General Cox is weary and ragged, a man on the edge of collapse.

FB: This is outrageous! Who do you think you are?

SAMUELS: Sir!

FB: Excuse me?

SAMUELS: "Who do you think you are, sir!" That's General Cox you're talking to, and he thinks he's General Cox. So do I.

GENERAL COX: Shut up, Samuels. I apologize for the intrusion, Mr. . . .

FB: Carter. Fountain Branch Carter.

GENERAL COX: Mr. Carter. I'm afraid the United States require the use of your home.

FB: The use of my home?

MARY ALICE: We're already using it!

SAMUELS: Not no more!

GENERAL COX: Shut up, Samuels! My army has marched through the night from Spring Hill. We need to delay here a few hours before we cross the Harpeth River and press toward Nashville.

                 I only require a temporary command post. No more than a few hours of your time.

FB: Is there going to be a fight?

GENERAL COX: Not if I can help it.

MARY ALICE: Then why are there cannons in the potato patch?

GENERAL COX: We only need to rest here until the bridge is ready. I expect we'll be gone by noonday.

MARY ALICE: They have no right, Papa. Don't stand for it.

SAMEULS: Don't you sass the general. *He* won't stand for it!

GENERAL COX: Shut up, Samuels.

MARY ALICE: My Lord! There must be a hundred men in the front yard!

GENERAL COX: I'm afraid there are twenty thousand men in your front yard.

MARY ALICE: Twenty thousand!?

Everyone runs to the windows to look out.

MINT JULEP: Quite a sight to see. The entire population of Franklin, Tennessee, numbered only 750 people. And here were nineteen brigades of Union soldiers. And no one's yet seen General Hood's twenty thousand rebels charging up Columbia Pike with fire in their eyes.

GENERAL COX: Including artillery that's better than forty thousand men.

MINT JULEP: It's a terrible thing to wake a body up of a morning.

Callie enters.

CALLIE: Marse Carter! They's a whole bunch of something going on. Look like somebody riled up a fight. A whole mess of cannons rolled by the other side the kitchen and—

FB: It's all right, Callie. Go and look after the children. There's nothing to worry about.

MARY ALICE: Fetch your biddies in here with mine. The poor things will be scared to death.

Mary Alice and Callie exit. General Cox seats himself at the desk Samuels has set up for him and he begins writing while Samuels inspects everything in the room as if window shopping.

FB: General, I assume you are a father yourself?

GENERAL COX: Yes. Six children.

FB: And when did you last see them?

GENERAL COX: It's been . . . some time. Too long.

FB: My wife is gone ten years now. My boy is gone to
                 fight in the war and hasn't been home in nearly
                 three years.

GENERAL COX: My boys are too young for it. And I'm thankful
                 every day. I'm sorry, Mr. Carter.

                 Believe me when I tell you I have no desire for
                 a fight. I've seen quite enough of it. We all have.
                 And if I could put an end to all this today, I tell
                 you I would do it.

                 This place has no strategic significance, and I
                 wouldn't care to shed a drop of blood in it's
                 defense. No offense to your home, you under-
                 stand. But we are bound north, Mr. Carter, to
                 join up with General Thomas.

                 They say we are here to preserve the Union, as
                 I'm sure you've heard. But I will be honest, I am
                 weary of its preservation. The best I can muster
                 right now is to get these men to Nashville.

                 You have my word that we will be no more
                 trouble to you than we must.

FB: Last year a house not three miles from here was—
                 was taken advantage of by your army, sir. Women
                 mistreated. A barn burned. Stores ransacked.

GENERAL COX: It pains me to hear of it, Mr. Carter.

FB: This house, this farm is our life . . .

GENERAL COX: An army marches on its belly, Mr. Carter, and at present mine finds itself hungry. I've given the men leave to take what they need. If you wish to look to the protection of your property, I suggest you do so.

FB: I see, but—

GENERAL COX: I could do with a meal. Do you think you could tell that slave girl of yours to bring me something?

FB: What? Well, yes, I could but—

GENERAL COX: And coffee too. If you'll excuse me, Mr. Carter, I've a missive to write. And I'd like to post a letter to my wife while I have a moment.

SAMUELS: And tell her bring me a biscuit too.

GENERAL COX: Shut up, Samuels. Was there anything else, Mr. Carter?

FB exits. The General sits at the desk and writes.

GENERAL COX: Here. Take this to Colonel Opdyke. And let me know as soon as that scout is back with news of the bridge. You said he knew the area, didn't you?

SAMUELS: Yes sir. He been all over it his whole life.

GENERAL COX: Good, then he shouldn't be long in coming. You're dismissed.

Samuels exits.

Now alone, the General takes off his hat and saber and relaxes somewhat. He takes up his pen again and writes.

Pounding at the door again.

GENERAL COX: Can a man find no peace?

The General continues writing while FB opens the door and Albert and Retha Lotz enter.

ALBERT: Where is he?

FB: Where is who?

ALBERT: There he is! You!

GENERAL COX: Are you the scout?

ALBERT: Scout!? I am no scout. Are you the one respon-
               sible for this . . . this madness?

Albert points an accusatory finger at General Cox and the scene freezes.

MINT JULEP: Albert Lotz. He and Retha come here from
               Germany a few years back, and he built that
               house just across yonder. When FB sold him the
               lot, it wasn't nothing but a few weeds and a tree
               full of raccoon. But now look. Bully if it ain't the
               handsomest house in Williamson County—

ALBERT: Or it was before the someone decided to pillage
               it.

MINT JULEP: Albert's a master carpenter, the finest in town.
               And that's not just his house, it's his showcase,
               his livelihood. Or it was.

The scene resumes.

ALBERT: My home is being torn apart! I tell them to stop
               and they laugh. I tell them to wait and they

laugh. I show them the deed to my land that I bought from FB Carter and they tell me to go show it to the general!

RETHA: Albert bought the land. You cannot take it. It is not yours. Tell him, FB.

FB: This is just what I was afraid of, General. You come in with a sweet enough tongue, but it's not half a day before it's all gone sour.

ALBERT: Do you have any idea how many hours I have spent building that house!

Tell him, FB. Tell him that it is my home!

GENERAL COX: No one is taking your home, sir, or your land.

FB: Perhaps you'd better go out there and tell your men that, General.

Calm down, Albert. I'm sure you're house will be fine.

GENERAL COX: Believe me, gentlemen. I respect the delicacy of the situation. But the men have been ordered to set up a defensive line while we—

FB: Wait a minute now. Why do they need a defensive line if there isn't going to be a fight?

ALBERT: A fight? What?

RETHA: Here?

GENERAL COX: We have no desire for a fight, but just as you look after your families, I look after my men and take measures to see they are protected.

Orders have been given, and they will be followed. I'm sorry if it causes you any inconvenience

ALBERT: Inconvenience?

Sir, if you want a proper fortification, I will be happy to build you one. And I will build one finer than what's being made of my front porch right now.

GENERAL COX: Then perhaps the best use of your time is to direct my men toward better use of what you have available.

General Cox dismisses the conversation and sits.

ALBERT: So this is the way of it in your country?

FB: No. No it is not. You go on, Albert. You too, Miss Retha. You'd best get your valuables and put them in my cellar. They'll be safe down there.

ALBERT: Thank you, FB.

RETHA: Thank you, FB.

FB: And maybe he's right. Maybe it's better to help them than to hinder.

ALBERT: I will do what I can.

Scene 9

Another pounding at the door. FB answers.

DELIVERY BOY: My lord, Mr. Carter. They sure is a passel of folks in the yard.

GENERAL COX: Are you the scout?

DELIVERY BOY: Scout? No, sir. I just come to see Mr. Carter.

GENERAL COX: Let me know at once when my scout arrives.

DELIVERY BOY: Was that a general?

FB: Apparently so.

DELIVERY BOY: I seen all them yanks outside, but I didn't expect to see no general. What's he doing, Mr. Carter? Ya'll all right?

FB: What do you want?

DELIVERY BOY: Got this here letter, sir. Got your name on it.

FB: Thank you.

Delivery Boy exits.

FB tears the letter open. Mary Alice enters. FB paces as he reads the letter silently.

MARY ALICE: What is it, Papa?

FB: It's Tod.

MARY ALICE: Tod?

FB: "To My Beloved Family."

MINT JULEP: It will please you to know that I've been granted furlough to visit you all. I shall leave as soon as I am able. Expect my arrival on the 30th of November. Give my love to Mary Alice. I hope to dine with you at your table and assuage any grief I have caused.

We shall soon be reunited.

FB: "Theodrick Carter."

MARY ALICE: November 30th? But that's . . .

MINT JULEP: *(to the audience)* Today.

MARY ALICE: But what does it mean? Papa?

FB: No, no, no . . .

FB paces and looks out the windows. The scene freezes.

MINT JULEP: When a boy goes off to war, it's not long before he gets to dreaming of home.

He dreams of a home-cooked dinner. A soft feather bed. A good day's work on his own land. And a house filled with smiling faces and ringing laughter.

Add to all that a boy's dream of a father's pride.

But in dreams of coming home, no one imagines he'll arrive to scene like this one.

An army between the boy and his father's table, and another army at his back.

What's a boy to do?

What's a father to say?

The scene resumes.

MARY ALICE: Papa?

FB: My boy is on the far side of twenty thousand Yankees. But the sooner they get across that bridge, the sooner they'll be gone, and the sooner he can come home. General? General!

My boy is out there. Do you hear? Out there.

GENERAL COX: I see. I am sorry, Mr. Carter.

FB: I must ask you and your men to leave. We've got to get the place cleaned up. Mary Alice, see that his bed is made. Callie, fetch the fattest turkey in the flock. General, I don't mean to be inhospitable, but my boy is coming home and you must give way.

GENERAL COX: Mr. Carter, you have my word that we will depart the moment we are able. I expect the crossing to begin any time now. I'm sure your boy is fine— and I'm sure he will be.

FB: You misunderstand me, sir. I am not making a request.

MARY ALICE: Papa, calm down.

GENERAL COX: I understand your position, Mr. Carter. Truly, I
               do.

FB: Good. Then I'll bid you good day and wish you
               and your men well.

GENERAL COX: It is not my intention to act harshly, sir.

FB: Nor mine.

MARY ALICE: Why don't we have some coffee. I'm sure Callie
               has some brewed. Would either of you like a
               cup?

GENERAL COX: Mr. Carter, we are men of good will, are we not?
               Men of reason?

MARY ALICE: Come with me into the kitchen, Papa.

FB: Men of reason? Does a man of reason enter
               where he has no welcome? Does he command
               where he has no authority? Does he eat what he
               has not sown? No, sir. I catch no scent of reason
               in this, only a base tyranny.

MARY ALICE: Papa, please!

*Pounding at the door. Mary Alice throws it open while FB and
General Cox stare at one another. Samuels rushes in.*

SAMUELS: General Cox, I just seen—

GENERAL COX: Miss Mary, I would be glad of that cup of coffee.
               Perhaps when we've had a drink, our heads will
               have cleared. Don't you think so, Mr. Carter.

FB fumes, but holds his tongue.

GENERAL COX: You were saying, Samuels?

SAMUELS: Scout's coming back, sir. I just seen him round
              the bend at a gallop.

GENERAL COX: Send word to Colonel Opdyke. Tell him to ready
              his men. We'll stay in position here and follow
              them once they're across the river.

SAMUELS: There's someone else, sir. A courier from General
              Wagner.

The courier bursts through the door, out of breath.

COURIER: General Cox, sir!

GENERAL COX: Are you the scout?

SAMUELS: He ain't the scout, he's General Wagner's man.

GENERAL COX: What is it son?

COURIER: The whole Army of Tennessee.

GENERAL COX: How's that?

COURIER: It's all of em, sir. Forest's cavalry is running
              skirmishes, and General Hood is coming right
              behind him. Look like he got every reb from
              here to Texas on his heels.

The scene freezes and Mint Julep addresses the audience.

MINT JULEP: Allow me to paint you a picture. Imagine for a
              moment a grizzly-bearded, one-legged, bear of a
              man named John Bell Hood. General of a mighty
              horde of rebel soldiers, the Army of Tennessee.
              Thanks to the audacity of a Yank at Little Round
              Top, he didn't even have but one working arm,

but he made up for it with a reckless nature that put terror into his adversaries. Imagine a man so fierce for battle that he bade his men strap him atop his horse so he could ride forth with them bravely despite the state of his mangled body.

GENERAL COX: That very man was beaten back by Sherman in Atlanta.

MINT JULEP: And in what some account a lunatic rage he set his sights on Nashville instead, the sacking of which is the last hope of confederate victory.

GENERAL COX: But if he's to have that victory, he will first have to destroy the men camped outside this house before we can reach the city and reinforce it beyond all hope of destruction.

MINT JULEP: Not more than a few hours ago, General Hood cornered them south of here in Spring Hill. He rode out and assured his men, that come the dawn they would annihilate General Cox and his entire army, and then ride for Nashville itself to claim the keys of victory.

GENERAL COX: But in the night, the Union army slipped quietly past them all.

MINT JULEP: Think of that! A whole army of Union soldiers marching by tip-toe in the dead of night. They must have held their breath to have moved so quietly past.

GENERAL COX: And come morning, General John Bell Hood awoke and looked out upon no more than a field of missed opportunity.

MINT JULEP: So now he's come a running, and don't you know
                 he's as angry as a hound after a wily rabbit.

The scene resumes.

SAMUELS: You reckon he's raring for a fight, general?

GENERAL COX: I expect he's the incarnation of Ares himself.

SAMUELS: He's what?

COURIER: General Wagner set up a defensive line to hold
                 him at Winstead Hill, but sir, he beg me tell you
                 he ain't going to hold long against all them rebs.

GENERAL COX: Tell Wagner he's needed in support here. You
                 boys are sitting ducks on that hill. Pull back
                 and reinforce our breastworks. Go, son. Double
                 quick.

*Pounding at the door. Samuels answers. Henry enters, dressed in a
Union uniform.*

MARY ALICE: Henry!

FB: Henry? It can't be.

HENRY: Morning, Miss Mary. Mister Carter.

GENERAL COX: Are you the scout?

FB: Scout? He's no scout. He's mine. He ran off a
                 year back and we haven't seen him since. Henry,
                 where have you been?

HENRY: Yes, sir. Lieutenant Samuels ask me go look over
                 the river.

GENERAL COX: And is the bridge in place?

HENRY: Sir, it ain't nothing there.

GENERAL COX: How's that? Speak up! What do you mean?

FB: What's going on here, Henry?

HENRY: It just ain't nothing there, sir. No bridge. No pontoons. No nothing but a couple boys trying to pull out catfish for they dinner.

GENERAL COX: Can we ford it on foot?

FB: What are you talking about?

GENERAL COX: Speak up, boy. You're talking to a general officer!

FB: Now look here. I don't know what's going on, but don't you talk to Henry that way. He's mine.

HENRY: No, sir. I ain't yours no more. I jine the army now.

GENERAL COX: And you'll be out of the army quick if you don't answer my question, private. Can we ford the river on foot?

HENRY: No, sir. The river's up bad. I wouldn't trust a fish to get crossed it for another couple days.

GENERAL COX: What's your name, boy?

HENRY: Private Carter, sir.

GENERAL COX: Private Carter, you hightail it back to that river and find those pontoons. Samuels, tell Opdyke to keep his position. Send for Captain Bridges. I want his batteries ready to fire if Hood gets jumpy.

SAMUELS: Yes, sir.

FB: Keep his position? You said you and your men would leave by noon!

GENERAL COX: That boy was a slave of yours?

FB: He still is. And he's a good boy. I raised him like my own.

GENERAL COX: Well, he's mine now, it would appear, and I'm sorry, Mr. Carter.

FB: What do you mean you're sorry?

GENERAL COX: It seems there is no bridge.

FB: No bridge? But . . .

GENERAL COX: We may have to stay a while longer. And I fear General Hood may take advantage.

FB: Take advantage? Take advantage of what?

GENERAL COX: Keep your family someplace safe. And pray Private Carter finds me my bridge. We are trapped here until he does.

Scene 10

Mint Julep saunters out.

MINT JULEP: We do make our choices, don't we? We raise a flag, we run from home, we sign our names to a cause, always expecting the small choice will make a big difference in the world.

But mostly they make their differences in us.

For some they are moments of resolve, moments when boys become men, they may even become heroes or legends. For others they're moments of blindness or pride, when boys realize they've strayed too far and can no longer find a way home.

Little by little they make up a life. We have to stand apart to see that the small, first choices, are shaping the choices to come. We think we're making them, but all the while, they're making us.

So then I ask you, are were fated men, or are we free?

I just now saw General Hood with a twinkle in his eye as they was strapping him onto his horse.

A fine, thing, yes sir. Yanks backed up against a river, and here's the Army of Tennessee, all got up proper and raring for a fight.

And where's that Tod Carter? As always, in the thick of it.

Mint Julep is buckling on his saber.

SOLDIER 1:   What you need that for, Cap'n? Thought the general sent you home?

MINT JULEP: That he did.

SOLDIER 1:   Well if he told me I could go home, he wouldn't have to tell me twice. Why you still hanging around here?

MINT JULEP: Because home is right where we're headed.

The soldier looks off into the distance.

SOLDIER 1:   You mean that little town yonder?

MINT JULEP: Franklin, Tennessee. Born and raised.

SOLDIER 1:   You know they got a whole Union army sitting on top of it, Cap'n. Come on and sit this one out. We'll have 'em cleared out by dinner.

MINT JULEP: My house is up there on that hill. If you look close you can see a battery of cannons sitting outside the kitchen window. There used to be a garden off to the left, and a grove of apple trees. My father planted them, and I climbed their branches when I was a boy and plucked down apples just to taste of their sweetness.

SOLDIER 1:   We had pears and peaches back on my daddy's farm.

MINT JULEP: And do you see that garden now, sergeant?

SOLDIER 1:   Can't see much from this distance.

MINT JULEP: The Union army has cut down the trees of my youth and piled them against us. Those apples are no more today than an abatis of barbs and skewers. The garden is planted with cannon. And my father's house is possessed by a legion of blue-coated tyrants.

And you ask me to sit this one out.

SOLDIER 2:   You got leave to stay in the rear, Cap'n. You can go home once we got 'em whipped.

SONG: "RUN, RUN, RIVER (TOD'S VERSION)"

SOLDIER 2:   Yeah, go on, Cap'n. We'll whup these Yanks for you. We'll have them put down by bedtime.

MINT JULEP: On the contrary, sergeant, no force on earth will keep me from this fight.

Mint Julep draws his saber.

Ready yourselves. Fix your bayonets. Raise your rebel yell. Say, brothers, are you with me? We are almost home.

SONG: "RUN, RUN, RIVER (TOD'S VERSION) (REPRISE)"

ACT II

SCENE 1

Campfire. Soldiers are playing instruments. Singing. Mint Julep rises.

SONG: "SAY, BROTHERS" (CONFEDERATES)

SAY, BROTHERS, WILL YOU MEET US?
SAY, BROTHERS, WILL YOU MEET US?
SAY, BROTHERS, WILL YOU MEET US?
ON CANAAN'S HAPPY SHORE.

Mint Julep: Say brothers, do you hear that? I think the Yanks are calling back!

From offstage.

SONG: "BATTLE HYMN" (YANKS)

GLORY, GLORY HALLELUJAH
GLORY, GLORY HALLELUJAH
GLORY, GLORY HALLELUJAH
HIS TRUTH IS MARCHING ON

The songs continue in a hum.

Mint turns to address the audience as a group of Yankee soldiers, including Henry, enter.

MINT JULEP: Now here's a peculiar thing. Of a time, we'd find ourselves so close to Billy Yank that we'd hear him singing 'round his own fire same as we're singing 'round ours. And was our songs so different?

HENRY: How could they be? We come up in the same houses.

MINT JULEP: Come up in the same churches, the same hills . . .

HENRY: . . . the same fields and rivers.

MINT JULEP: We were people of the same songs, just as we were of the same land. And what was it we dreamed of and sang for and hoped at last to find? That too was one and the same, though we saw it all through the crooked glass of our own pride.

                Are you with me, brothers?

The song continues in the round.

SONG: "SAY BROTHERS" / "BATTLE HYMN" ROUND

MINT JULEP: Strange ain't it? We go to war over everything we've got different between us, and then we stumble into peace when we recall what we've got in common. Peace for a moment at least. Sing it together, brothers.

The two camps sing together until a bugle sounds, interrupting. Mint Julep watches both camps gather their arms and march off-stage.

MINT JULEP: It was fine while it lasted, but there they go. Same as they always do.

GENERAL COX: They march off toward their destinies, wrapped up in fear and homesickness, hatred and righteousness.

HENRY: Thousands of them will be gone before the sun sets.

MINT JULEP: Others will never get shut of what they see today, and what they do, and what's done in return.

GENERAL COX: Every one of them is a ball of hopes and fears about to be packed into a cannon and shot off into a distant fury.

MINT JULEP: Every time I come here, I hope the bugle will keep its silence and let us sing on and on.

HENRY: But it doesn't, does it?

GENERAL COX: The song always gives way to the bugle.

MINT JULEP: Perhaps there will come a day when the bugle gives way to the song.

SCENE 2

Carter House. Soldiers busy as bees, back and forth, building forti-fications.

FB: Mary Alice!

MARY ALICE: Papa, what is it?

FB: Where are the children.

MARY ALICE: They are upstairs in the bedroom. The girls
             are scared half to death and the boys are in
             a fit because they want to go out and see the
             cannons.

FB: Get everyone into the cellar.

MARY ALICE: The cellar?

FB: We should be safe in the cellar if there's . . . if
             there's trouble.

MARY ALICE: A battle? Lord a mercy, Papa. Here? What about
             Tod.

FB: Where's Callie?

CALLIE: Right here, Marse Carter. You say there goan be a battle?

FB: You best gather up the rest of the darkies and find someplace to weather it.

CALLIE: Where's my Henry gone, sir? Was it him? Was it really him? Where you send him? He ain't gone is he?

FB: It was Henry, yes. But he's—he's betrayed us. You best forget about him.

CALLIE: Betrayed us?

FB: I raised that boy like he was my own! And what does he do? Run off? Oh ho, and not just run off, but joined the Union army!

CALLIE: He done what?

FB: He's dead to me. And he's dead to you too, you hear! Forget him. You go get hid.

CALLIE: Marse Carter, don't talk like that. My Henry cain't be dead to you and not to me neither. And where we goan go? The soldiers done tear down our house for wood.

FB: You best go get Albert. He hasn't got a cellar. Tell him to bring his family over here.

CALLIE: What about my family.

FB: Go on and do like I told you, Callie.

CALLIE: Yes, sir.

FB and Mary Alice exit. Callie departs and discovers Henry outside.

CALLIE: Henry? Henry, wait!

HENRY: My lord but you a sight for sore eyes, Callie.

CALLIE: Is you a ghost, Henry? Or is you real? Marse
               Carter tole me you was dead to us. But it cain't
               be, can it?

HENRY: I ain't dead, Callie. I jine the army, jest like you
               said. Pay me sixteen dollar a month, same as a
               white man.

CALLIE: Take us with you, Henry. I can't stand it for you
               to be gone no more.

HENRY: I cain't, Callie. I got to go scout for the general.
               But I'll be back directly. They say the rebs itching
               to put up a fight, so you best get somewhere safe
               fore it start.

CALLIE: But you never been no fighting man, Henry. I
               know I tole you to go, but now I seen it, I cain't
               stand it. You ain't going to fight are you?

HENRY: Used to I done like Marse Carter said. But now I
               got to do like the general say. Maybe the general
               tell me to go fight. Maybe he tell me to go scout.
               I don't know. Most time they jest tell me go
               work—same as Marse Carter done.

               "Load that wagon, Henry. Pack that tent, Henry.
               Wash them dishes, Henry."

               Maybe one day I come back and do like no body
               but me says. That'd be fine, wouldn't it? But right
               now I got to go see that river, Callie. All these
               boys got to get to the other side.

CALLIE: Look at me now, Henry. And you listen to me.
               You do like I say, you hear? You go do what you
               got to do, and then you come back. You gone
               away enough, and now you got to come back.
               You chirren got to see they father. You wife got
               to see her husband. She got to hold on to him.
               You hear me?

HENRY: You reckon I done good, Callie?

CALLIE: I reckon you done so, so good.

HENRY: I sure run off, ain't I?

CALLIE: You sure did.

HENRY: And I got free, ain't I?

CALLIE: You sure has. You ain't no body but you own
               now. So you go do like that general tole you, and
               then you come back, Henry Carter. You hear?

HENRY: I got to go find that bridge.

CALLIE: I know. But you come back, Henry. You hear?

Henry departs.

CALLIE: You hear?

                SONG: "HE'S ALL THAT I HAVE OF MY OWN"

Scene 3

Carter House.

General Cox: Samuels! My eyes aren't what they used to be. Look out there and tell me what you see.

Samuels: A bunch of rebs lined up for a fight.

General Cox: Does it look to you like General Wagner's division is dug in?

Samuels: They're dug in all right. And they look a bit skittish, sir. Look mighty small out there.

General Cox: Dammit. I told him to pull back.

Get on my horse and ride down there as fast as you can. Tell Wagner to fall back and support our position here.

Samuels: Yes, sir!

General Cox: Go, quickly.

Samuels: Sir?

General Cox: What is it?

SAMUELS: Too late, general.

GENERAL COX: What? Why?

Samuels points. Bugles sound in the distance.

GENERAL COX: My god.

Musket fire in the distance.

> Hood is attacking. Tell Bridges to have his artillery ready to fire in support. Wagner's no hope of holding that line. He'll have to retreat, and when he does Hood will be at his heels. Go, Samuels. Tell them.

FB and Mary Alice enter followed by Albert and Retha.

ALBERT: This is not good, FB. Not good.

> But we're safe in here with the general, yes? Ah, I see it now! That is why you let him stay here!

FB: Let him stay?! I've done no such thing! I've had no say in the matter whatsoever!

ALBERT: Whoa! Easy, FB!

FB: He's taken my home too, or hadn't you noticed! He's turned my darkies against me, and now he aims to have a battle when he knows my boy is out there—on the other side.

RETHA: Tod? Tod's out there?

MARY ALICE: We had a letter from him this morning. But we don't know he's out there, now do we, Papa. Don't mind, him. He's upset.

FB: Upset is scarcely the word for it. I'm undone.

ALBERT: But we'll be safe here, won't we?

MARY ALICE: I expect so. The general wouldn't be here if it wasn't safe—would he?

Callie: All the chirren down in the basement, Miss Mary.

An eruption of musketfire in the distance. Samuels enters.

SAMUELS: General Cox!

GENERAL COX: *(Looking through his spyglass)* I see it. I see it. Tell Bridges to fire as soon as they can get over our boys' heads. And tell the line to hold its fire until Wagner is inside the perimeter.

Samuels exits again.

FB: What's going on?

MARY ALICE: *(Looking out the window)* God help us!

ALBERT: They're coming right this way!

GENERAL COX: Everyone, take cover! Now!

OFFSTAGE: "FIRE!"

Cannons erupt.

MINT JULEP: *(Whistles)* What a sight to see. Just about a quarter mile down that away, out in front of the Union line, sits General Wagner and a division of over 3000 Yanks. And beyond him? General Hood and 20,000 angry rebels.

That's nearly ten rebs to every Billy Yank of Wagner's. And what do you think happened when those rebs charged?

That's right. *Pow.* Look you right yonder. I see General Wagner's division—which is to say what's left of it—running right this way.

GENERAL COX: They're in full retreat, coming for shelter behind the main Union line.

MINT JULEP: Those poor boys are praying the earth itself will cover them up and hide them from the wrathful hounds at their heels.

BOOM! Cannons.

Hear that? That's Union artillery. Twelve pound cannon balls punching holes the size of horses in the wave of rebels coming across yonder field. It's a fearful thing, ain't it? Awful to hear, and even awfuller to see.

And maybe you're asking yourself right now, where's that Tod Carter in all this?

Scene 4

Rebel soldiers enter and Mint joins them.

Soldier 1:   Form ranks! Fix bayonets! Load!

Soldier 2:   We got 'em on the run boys. We charge straight on and we don't stop until we've pushed them into the river. Can we do that?

Soldiers answer with cheers.

Soldier 2:   Cap'n Carter? We're ready.

Mint Julep: Very good, sergeant. I believe we have some work to do.

Cheers.

Soldier 2:   The boys are all formed up, sir. Just waiting for the command.

Mint Julep: Very good, lieutenant. I'll lead the charge.

Soldier 2:   You will, sir?

Mint Julep: I'll lead this charge—and I'll not quit the field until I gain the house atop that hill.

Are you with me, brothers?

Follow me! We are almost home, boys!

The bugle sounds and the men charge.

MINT JULEP: And there they go. What do you think they're charging into? Victory? History? Songs? Legends? Charging into eternity? Perhaps. But most assuredly, they are running to greet a great hell of fire, blood, hatred, and rage.

GENERAL COX: And it will consume them.

Scene 5

Carter House. Cannon and musket fire. Henry enters.

HENRY: General!

CALLIE: Henry!

Callie runs to Henry and embraces him.

GENERAL COX: You have news of the bridge?

HENRY: Yes, sir. They bringing the pontoons, sir, but the river's up so high they having a hard time of it. They say they be ready in few hours.

GENERAL COX: Hours!? We don't have a few hours.

Samuels bursts in.

SAMUELS: General! You seeing this?

GENERAL COX: My God!

The scene freezes.

MINT JULEP: What he just saw is a sight to chill any general's blood. Not a hundred yards down the hill, right there, is the front line of the Union army.

And coming this way is a tidal wave of grey steel and hot lead. That's General Hood bringing the hammer down.

His rebs are charging at Wagner's heels, following on them so close that the Union boys can't even fire until Hood's men are a mere breath away.

Think of it! Here they come! Hearts beating. Blood pounding. A ragged cry in every throat. A breath. A moment of eerie quiet and—FIRE!—perdition erupts like a volcano.

Entire companies disappear from the face of the earth, obliterated in a rush of gnashing teeth and flying lead coughed forth from the steely throats of ten thousand guns.

Hood's men are being ground to pieces, but the the Union line is shattered right down the middle.

It's as if the devil has taken full possession of the earth.

The scene resumes.

GENERAL COX: Samuels, tell Opdyke to bring his brigade up and plug that breach in the line!

SAMUELS: Sir?

GENERAL COX: The whole center has collapsed and they are about to cut us in half. Go, Samuels!

Go now, or we die!

SAMUELS: Yes, sir.

Samuels opens the door and is immediately shot dead.

GENERAL COX: No!

General Cox shakes Samuels' body, then looks around in desperation.

HENRY: I'll go, sir.

CALLIE: Henry, no!

FB: You'll do no such thing, Henry.

GENERAL COX: Go, private. Find Colonel Opdyke. Tell him I need him at the center. Go!

FB: You're a black traitor, Henry! Tod is out there!

CALLIE: Henry, don't go. You goan get killed. Stay here with me, Henry. Please.

HENRY: Sorry, Mister Carter, but I'm my own man now. I do hope Mister Tod be okay.

                Callie? You keep safe, hear?

CALLIE: Henry, no!

HENRY: I tell him, General.

GENERAL COX: Run, private! Run!

Henry departs.

Scene 6

Carter House. Relentless cannonfire.

FB: Into the cellar! Everyone!

Everyone but General Cox piles into the cellar.

CALLIE: Don't close the door, Marse Carter. Henry coming back and he need to get down here. He never been no fighting man.

FB: Forget Henry! I'll have nothing to do with him!

CALLIE: Henry ain't no traitor, sir. I tole him to do it. I tole him to run off. He done it cause of me, sir. Don't leave him out there cause of me. I can't bear it.

FB: Get off of me!

                This is the return I get for years of kindness? I treated you, all of you, like my own!

FB pushes Callie away.

CALLIE: Like you own? Like you *own*!?

FB: Yes! Like my own family. I treated Henry like a son!

CALLIE: How you treat us like you own, when you own ain't got to work till they hands bleed. How you treat us like you own when you own come as they please, go as they please. How you treat us like you own when you tell me he dead to you? If Henry is you own, don't close the door, Marse Carter. Don't you close the door! I won't let you!

FB raises his hand to Callie.

MARY ALICE: Papa!

CALLIE: We ain't you own and never has been. That's why I tole Henry run off. If he was you own, he don't have to run no where to get free.

MARY ALICE: Callie, come away. Henry's going to be fine. I know it.

FB: That boy is dead to me. I don't even want to hear his name.

MARY ALICE: He's not dead, Papa. Stop saying that! Stop it!

FB: Have you joined them now? Has everyone in my house turned against me? What about you, Albert? Have you got something to say?

MARY ALICE: Stop it, Papa! Have you ever thought that maybe it's not us? Maybe it's not them?

FB: I will not listen to this in my own home. I treated them like my own flesh and blood and . . .

MARY ALICE: Yes! Yes maybe you did! But how did you treat your own flesh and blood? You chased my brother away, Papa! Why do you think it is he doesn't write to you? Why do you think it is he hasn't come home in three years? You pushed him away from us!

FB: I loved that boy! And if he could not see it then it's his own blindness that prevented him.

MARY ALICE: How? How did you love him, Papa? Tell me how?

FB: I don't have to answer to you.

MARY ALICE: Tell me!

FB: I fed him! I taught him. I kept him safe! I gave my own sweat and blood for him. I built all this—for him!

MARY ALICE: But you never say it, Papa. You never say it. Look at me! Did you ever tell him? Did you ever tell Tod yourself? Did you ever tell him you saw him at all?

FB: Tell him? What do I have to tell him when I show him with every day of my life?

MARY ALICE: You got to say it, too, Papa. You got to say it. Why do you think he run off?

FB: Don't you dare blame me, Mary Alice. Don't you do it.

MARY ALICE: He wanted to please you, Papa. That's all he ever wanted. He wanted you to see him. He wanted you to see him and be proud of him.

FB: He had a peculiar way of showing it.

MARY ALICE: And where do you think he learned that? Are
                 you blind!

CALLIE: Don't close the door, Marse Carter. Henry
                 coming back.

MARY ALICE: Tod's out there too, Papa. Papa, please.

FB slams the door shut.

*The stage goes dark. Sounds of battle grow. Cannonfire. Screams.
Muskets.*

SCENE 7

Exterior. Mint Julep enters, followed by soldiers.

MINT JULEP: Move up! Move up!

Musket fire.

There's a breach!

The soldiers charge forward. Mint addresses the audience.

Twenty thousand men started across the field. We've charged nearly two miles, and here we are at last. There's not fifty yards between this spot and the Union line, and we've brought all hell with us.

Just through that breach is the Union headquarters where General Cox has surely felt the chill of defeat come to tickle his neck.

Let's put an end to it. Tod Carter is anxious for his homecoming.

Mint moves back to the scene.

Straight on, brothers. We're nearly there. Charge!

The soldiers charge offstage.

SCENE 8

Carter House. Union Soldiers stumble through the door in retreat, firing muskets.

SOLDIER 2:   We can't hold em, General. They've broken through.

SOLDIER 1:   Here they come!

Musket fire. One soldier falls dead. Rebel soldiers push through the door. Hand to hand fighting.

GENERAL COX: Fall back! Fall back!.

A rebels soldier yells and rushes General Cox. Henry enters and struggles with him, until General Cox draws his pistol and shoots the soldier. Bugles. Battle cries. Union soldiers rush past Henry and push the rebels out of the house.

HENRY: I tole you I could get him, sir.

GENERAL COX: What? Who?

HENRY: Colonel Opdyke, sir. I brung him to you. Look there.

Mint Julep steps forward.

MINT JULEP: What General Cox saw—and what General
                Hood could not foresee high atop his warhorse—
                was that from behind the Carter House, Colonel
                Emerson Opdyke and his brigade of Illinois
                regulars had leapt forth from their position in
                reserve. Had Hood known they were waiting
                there, would he have ordered the charge? Who
                can say. But he did. We all make our choices.

                Hood's rebels smashed the center of the Union
                line and drove a hole clean through it, but right
                in the moment of their push for certain victory—
                Opdyke's brigade pushed back. A hail of hellfire
                engulfed the Carter House and everyone in it.

Bugles. Cannons. Muskets.

GENERAL COX: By God, you've done it, Private Carter. Good
                man. Now, quickly, go see if you can find General
                Reilly. Tell him to come up and reinforce the
                right flank. Run!

HENRY: Yes, sir.

Henry runs to the basement door and pounds on it.

                Callie?

CALLIE: Henry? Henry, that you? Open the door, Marse
                Carter! Henry out there!

FB: Get away!

HENRY: You keep safe in yonder, Callie. Ya'll all keep safe.
                Don't come out till I tell you, you hear? Don't
                you come out less I tell you!

CALLIE: Henry! Henry!

GENERAL COX: Here they come again. Private, go!

Henry runs to the door, takes a look back, then opens it and runs out. The door slams closed and the stage goes dark again.

SCENE 9

The darkness of the basement. Sounds of battle.

ALBERT: We'll all be killed.

RETHA: Quiet, Albert. The children!

SOLDIER 2:   *(From offstage)* Look out!

SOLDIER 1:   *(offstage)* Fire!

Muskets. Screams. Cannons.

GENERAL COX: *(offstage)* On the right! Go! Go!

Scuffling.

MARY ALICE: My God! They're in the house! Papa!

Muskets. Screams. Hand to hand fighting outside. Pounding at the door.

FB: Albert! Help me!

FB and Albert brace the door.

SOLDIER 1:   *(From behind the door)* Open up. Let us in!

SOLDIER 2:   They're coming! Help us! Open the door.

Screams. Muskets.

CALLIE: *(screams)*

MARY ALICE: *(screams)*

FB and Albert struggle at the door.

SOLDIER 1:   Open the door! Open the door!

MARY ALICE: Papa, let them in! Let them in!

CALLIE: Maybe Henry out there! Open the door, Marse
                  Carter. I can't stand it no more!

FB: By God, they have taken all they will take of
                  mine! I have nothing left except what lives in this
                  room. They will not have it!

MARY ALICE: Papa, please! Please! What if it's Tod?

ALBERT: FB, perhaps we should . . .

FB: No! No! No one gets in!

SOLDIER 1:   Look out!

SOLDIER 2:   Let us in!

*Sounds of fighting. Muskets and cannons are relentless. Finally we
hear the soldiers outside killed and rebel yells erupt. The door stills.
Mary Alice weeps.*

CALLIE: Henry! Oh my sweet Jesus. My Henry!

MARY ALICE: Papa. Tod isn't out there is he? He can't be can
                  he?

FB: I don't know. I don't know. Don't touch me!
               Move back. Move back.

               What have I done? What have I done?

Mint Julep enters and watches as the family cowers in the darkness.

MINT JULEP: Hours. Hours in the dark while hell reigned
               in the land above. Men tore each other apart.
               Hacked at limbs with knives, stove in heads with
               shovels.

GENERAL COX: Cannons rent them.

MINT JULEP: Muskets spent them.

GENERAL COX: You never saw such rage and hate, such fear, and
               yes, such gallantry and courage.

MINT JULEP: Does one balance the other?

GENERAL COX: Who can tell?

MINT JULEP: Boys were shot right there on the doorstep.

GENERAL COX: They grappled and stabbed each other and bled
               out their short lives in the dirt.

MINT JULEP: A drummer boy from Mississippi died right
               there in the road. He never even fired a weapon.
               He was eat up with fear and driven onward
               because he was too scared to go anywhere else.
               When he died they trampled over his body as if
               no mother had ever loved him, and by the end he
               was no more than a puddle of mud.

GENERAL COX: Right down there General Cleburne drew his
               saber and urged his men forward, the very

picture of valor, until a musket ball tore through his heart.

MINT JULEP: And over there by that tree General Adams died storming the breastworks.

GENERAL COX: Right about here, General Hiram Granby fell, pierced by many wounds.

MINT JULEP: And there . . .

GENERAL COX: And there . . .

MINT JULEP: And there . . .

GENERAL COX: Another . . .

MINT JULEP: Another . . .

GENERAL COX: Another . . .

MINT JULEP: How do you tell the tale of it all? The ground itself cried out for mercy.

GENERAL COX: But the devil would give no quarter.

MINT JULEP: And all the while they waited in the darkness while the screams and shouts and shots echoed round about. And they wondered . . .

MARY ALICE: Where's Tod? Where's Tod?

The battle fades.

SCENE 10

SONG: "BATTLE OF FRANKLIN THEME" (HUMMED)

MINT JULEP: Sometime in the darkness, it was over. The cannons hushed, and the shots stopped, but the dying didn't. Men lay around the house by the hundreds, and the lucky were the dead. The rest went on dying all night long.

General Hood's valiant charge reaped only destruction. When the smoke cleared, his army had taken a mortal blow. The blood of 10,000 men had wetted the ground, and more than 7,000 of them were Hood's ragged confederates. From that day forward the Rebel Yell would be no more than the cry of a lost cause, the lament of a lost people.

And so did General Cox and his Yankees turn at last to the river.

Henry enters, showered in light.

HENRY: Mister Tod, that you?

MINT JULEP: Henry? Henry what are you doing here?

HENRY: I run off. Jest like we said we would—you
              remember?

MINT JULEP: You run off too? I'd nearly forgot.

HENRY: Run futher than I ever been.

MINT JULEP: Henry you got to go back. It ain't safe here. Pa
              will be needing you.

HENRY: No, sir. He cain't need me no more. It's you he
              need. Not me. And it always have been.

MINT JULEP: Me? Pa don't even like to look at me, most times.

HENRY: You got it all wrong, Mister Tod. Most always
              have. Your Pa love you 'cause you his own, and
              right now that's all he know how to love. You got
              to get on back to him.

MINT JULEP: It's too late for me, Henry. I been here before.
              Again and again, and it's always the same.

HENRY: Ain't too late, Mister Tod. That's what I come
              to tell you. It's always the same, but it's always
              different too. And you seeing me now, ain't you?

MINT JULEP: Why you wearing that uniform, Henry? You
              can't jine no army.

HENRY: But I done it, ain't I? Maybe I ain't no fighting
              man. Maybe I ain't no white man. But a body
              got to do something don't he? So his chirren
              ain't got to be somebody else's own? Yes, sir. I
              reckon they do. A body got to get up, got to run
              off, maybe got to go to hell 'fore he can get quit
              of his chains.

But I done it. I got rights now. I see 'em. They lights me up, Mister Tod. Shining. I see 'em clear as I see you. And now I seen em, I got to show em. I got to show em to Callie. You see? I got to show em to my chirren. Light 'em up. So they learn how to see they own . . . and then they don't never forget. No, sir. They remember then, thenceforward and forever.

MINT JULEP: You do look something different, Henry. Something different indeed.

HENRY: You shouldn't a left, Mister Tod. You shouldn't a left. But we all got to go back. We got to go back before we can go on and get to where we got to be.

MINT JULEP: I do want to go back, Henry. I surely do. But I can't see how to get there.

HENRY: But we see each other now, Mister Tod, and that's how we find the way. Cause soon we got to run off again.

MINT JULEP: Run off? Where to, Henry? Hell?

HENRY: Naw, we already been. And if I'm to run off, I aim to go someplace most folks ain't never seen. Say, brother, will you come with me?

MINT JULEP: I want to, Henry. I surely do. But I don't know if I can. I can't see how to get free of it all. I can't see . . .

I can't see . . .

General Cox enters, exhausted, bloody, checking the wounded and dead. Mint Julep steps into the shadows.

HENRY: You done good, sir.

GENERAL COX: What? Who's there?

HENRY: I said you done good, sir.

General Cox checks a body for life.

GENERAL COX: They tell me we are preserving the Union?

HENRY: Yes, sir.

GENERAL COX: Did you see those boys out there today? All the
                    thousands of them. I told them to go, and they
                    did. I told them to hold, and they did. I . . . I
                    ordered them to . . . they killed one another like
                    animals! Good boys. Gone. Poured out, like
                    water in a ditch.

                    Even Samuels.

HENRY: But you done it, sir.

GENERAL COX: If there was any union left in the world, I fear
                    I have killed it here today—and we shall all be
                    damned for its murder.

HENRY: No, sir. They's still hope.

                    You listen to me. You got to get on to Nashville.
                    They be needing you up there soon.

                    That bridge ready now.

                    They's a bridge clear to the other side. I cross
                    over just to be sure. It go all the way, and they's a
                    fair land over yonder, sir. I spect the catfish bite
                    better on that other bank. Yes, sir. I spect they
                    do.

GENERAL COX: This war has got to end, doesn't it? O God, grant
me a moment's rest. But not yet. Not yet.

*General Cox exits. Henry lingers, pulls the two halves of the torn
proclamation from his pocket, and reads them silently. Then he lies
down on the floor among the dead.*

*Mint straightens the room, as in the beginning. He pulls the bed
into the center and neatens it up. After appraising the room and
finding it satisfactory, he speaks.*

MINT JULEP: All as I remember it, yet new, as if seen for the
first time.

I'm ready.

Mint lies down.

*FB opens the door. The family comes out and looks around at the
house. Bodies everywhere.*

ALBERT: They've gone. They're all gone.

FB: Tod?

CALLIE: Where's my Henry?

Mary Alice sees Tod.

MARY ALICE: Tod? He's alive! Tod! Papa come quick!

FB: Son? Oh my son! My own. Help me.

CALLIE: Henry? Henry!

Callie looks frantically for Henry.

FB: What's happened to him? Do something? What
do I do?

MARY ALICE: He's shot, Papa. He's shot bad.

ALBERT: I'm afraid it's mortal. All we can do is make him comfortable.

CALLIE: Henry!

Callie finds Henry, dead, with the torn proclamation in his hand. She collapses in tears, wailing.

You cain't be dead, Henry. You cain't go. I got to hold onto you. Oh, Jesus, send him back, please send him back.

MARY ALICE: Tod? Tod stay with me. Are you with me? You're home now. Can you hear me?

FB: Someone get a—get a doctor. Bandages! Do we have bandages? What do I do? Help him. Tod! Come back to me! What must I say?

               What must I say?

MARY ALICE: My brother's come home at last. Lord, don't let him go again so soon! Don't let him go so soon! No. No. No. Brother, are you with me?

Callie mourns on one side of the stage. The Carter family on the other, facing away from one another. Mint Julep rises and faces the audience while the family mourns.

MINT JULEP: Here I am. Again. There I lay. Again. A memory renewed by the revolution of time.

               Is this the way it happened? Perhaps. Perhaps not. But this is the way the heart remembers it. Again and again and again, the same as it always is . . .

Mint sees Callie mourning, and Henry's body.

MINT JULEP: ... yet new.

> How is it we paid so little attention to one
> another. We could not see one another for who
> we were. We were strangers together in the same
> house, unseeing, unknowing, unloving.

*Henry rises and helps dead soldiers up off the battlefield, leading
them to the bridge.*

HENRY: You see it now, don't you, Mister Tod. You sees it
               clear.

MINT JULEP: If time could wind back this war and I could live
               at home in peace, I don't intend that anybody
               would make a better son than I, a better brother,
               a better friend.

               I would spend, with all these, many a happy day,
               if only this scourge would pass me over.

HENRY: That's it, Mister Tod. You shining now. I see it on
               you.

MINT JULEP: There will be a life beyond this vale of tears, won't
               there? A land where we will outlive all sorrow
               and gloom, where all shall be joy, and love, and
               peace?

HENRY: Now you with me, brother. Tell it.

Mint turns to his family.

MINT JULEP: I will see you in that blessed land where the
               weary are at rest, and where war shall trouble us
               no more.

HENRY: Yes, brother!

MINT JULEP: We shall be reunited, a family unbroken, if not in this land, then in that other.

HENRY: *(To Callie)* Thenceforward and forever.

MINT JULEP: *(To his family)* Thenceforward and forever.

(To Henry) Thenceforward and forever.

Mint turns back to the audience.

My end is in my beginning, but I shall make of my ending something new.

Time spins us 'round, through memory, through pain, and in these moments allows us grace enough to stand at the pinnacle from which we may survey the unshadowed valley beyond.

HENRY: I seen a river there. It run free and clear to the shining sea.

MINT JULEP: And that is why we come. Over and over, we remember again, hoping each time that we will climb high enough to catch a glimpse of the land we are tumbled ever toward. And with each glance from the mountaintop we learn to see that valley more clearly, to expect it more anxiously, and to take some part of it with us when we go.

HENRY: Bridge ready, Brother Tod. Time we gone on across.

MINT JULEP: Thank you, brother.

Time has allowed us to journey together for

only so far, and now it carries us along different streams into different histories and possibilities yet to be discovered.

You have been fine company, and I regret that we must part so soon.

SONG: "RUN, RUN, RIVER (REPRISE)"

Henry and Mint Julep walk to the bridge, then turn to watch.

MARY ALICE: He's gone, Papa. Tod's gone.

FB: Come back to me, son. Come back. Come back. Come back.

CALLIE: Henry!

MINT JULEP: Tomorrow we shall hope again that some happier homecoming reveals itself—and we shall not cease from our exploration until time itself falls still, and all shall be well, and all shall be well, and all manner of thing shall be well.

History is now. History is Franklin. But as for the present, I, Tod Carter, must bid you farewell.

SONG: "WE ARE CLIMBING JACOBS LADDER"

WE ARE CLIMBING JACOB'S LADDER
WE ARE CLIMBING JACOB'S LADDER
WE ARE CLIMBING JACOB'S LADDER
SOLDIERS OF THE CROSS

The cast crosses the bridge and exits. Henry and Mint wait until the last and cross the bridge together.

THE END.

Also from

Rabbit Room Press

The Last Sweet Mile
by Allen Levi

Everlasting Is the Past
by Walter Wangerin, Jr.

The World According to Narnia
by Jonathan Rogers

The Molehill (Vol. 1, 2, 3)
A Rabbit Room Miscellany

For more information, visit press.RabbitRoom.com.

RABBIT ROOM
— PRESS —

www.RabbitRoom.com

CPSIA information can be obtained
at www.ICGtesting.com
Printed in the USA
LVOW07*2012200817

545729LV00001BA/1/P